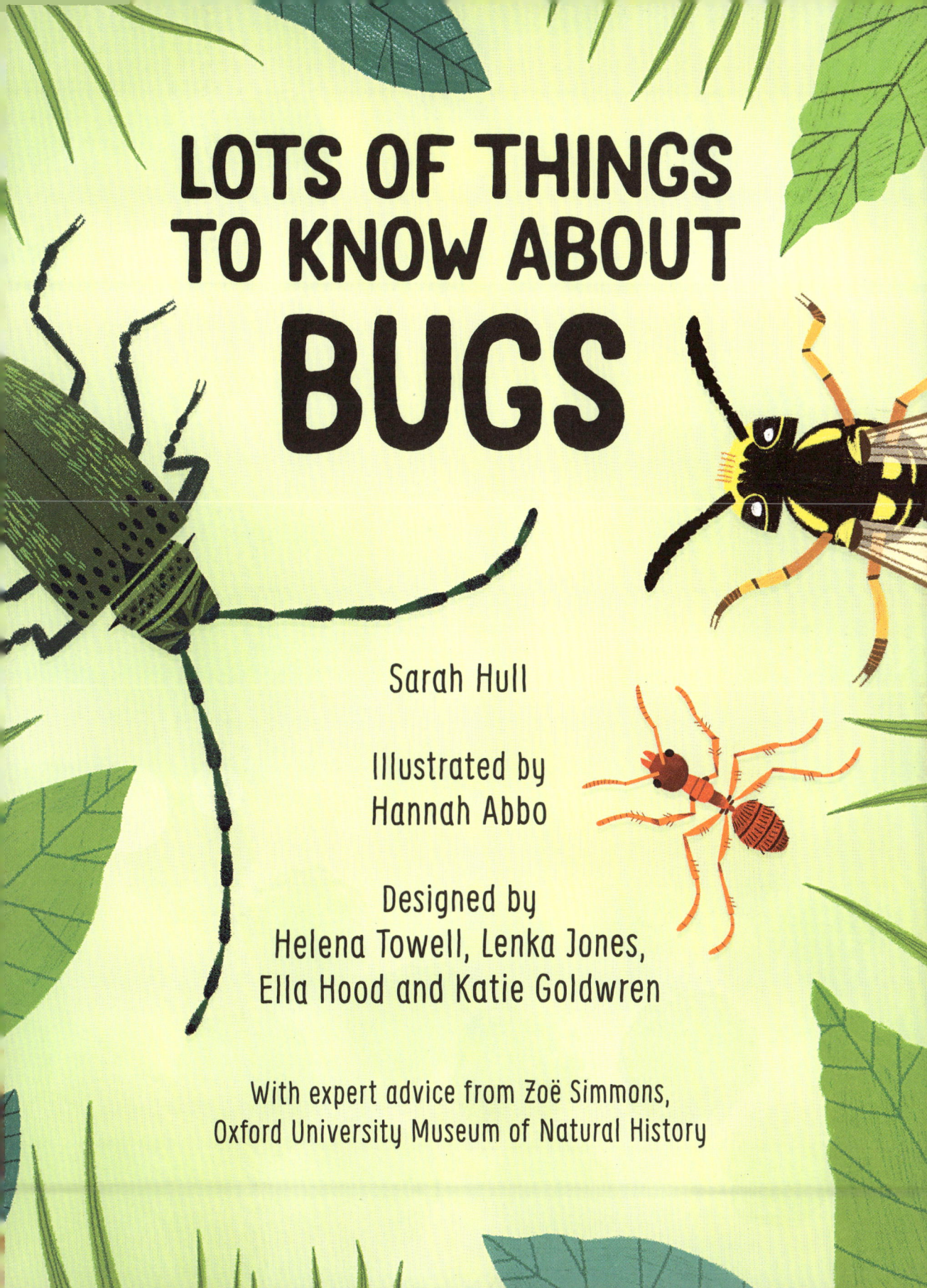

We're going on a bug hunt...

When people talk about bugs, they usually mean creeping, crawling, fluttering minibeasts. If you look closely, you'll find these amazing creatures all around.

GHOST MANTIS

Some look as weird as aliens...

PIPEVINE SWALLOWTAIL CATERPILLAR

BRAZILIAN TREEHOPPER

No one knows why I have a strange helicopter-like hat with four balls on my back.

We look like precious jewels!

TANSY BEETLE

You might not see any of the bugs on this page in the wild, but you're sure to see others that are in this book.

RAINBOW LEAF BEETLE

Are there lots of types of bugs?

Yes, I'll show you over the page.

3

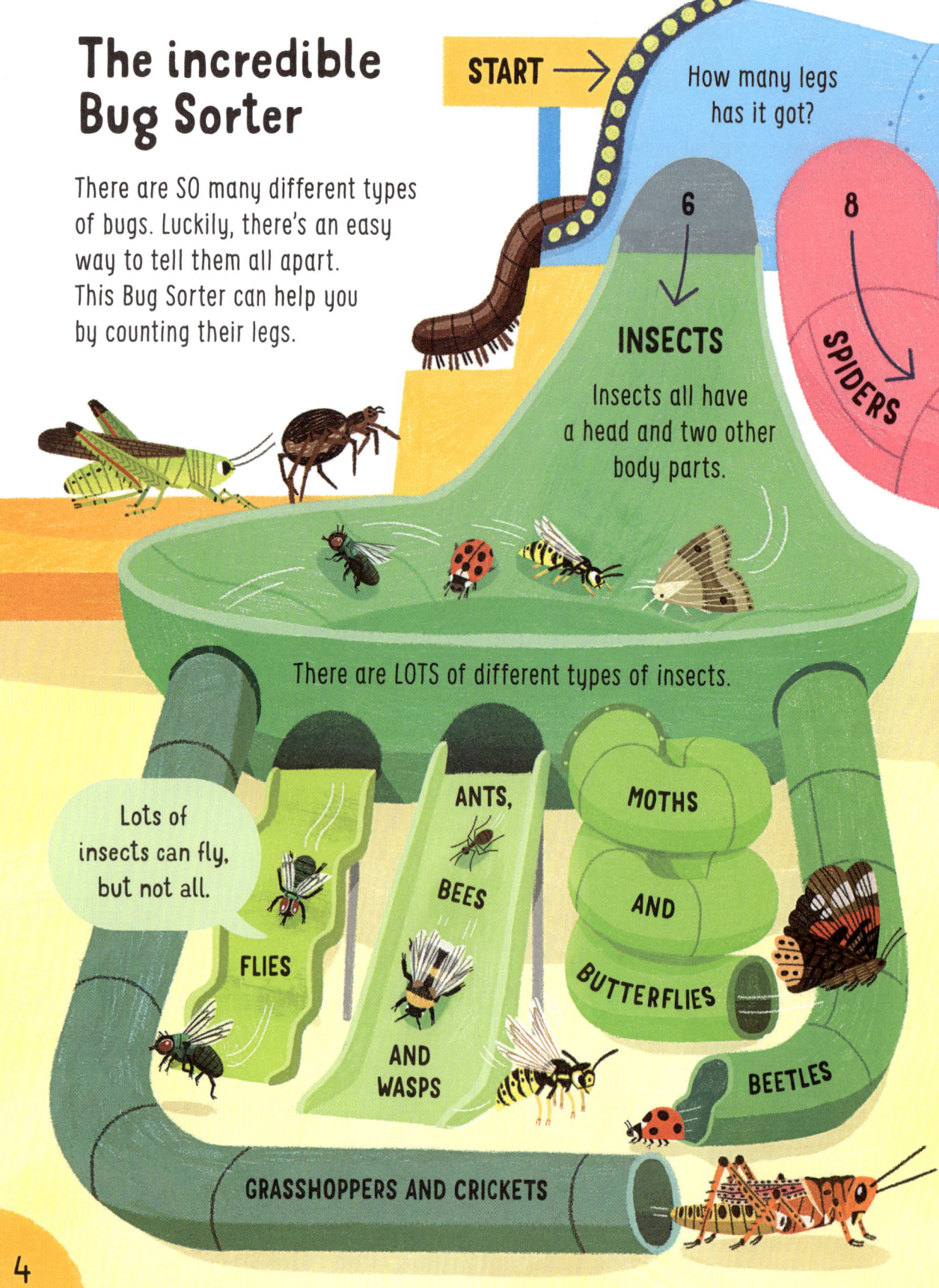

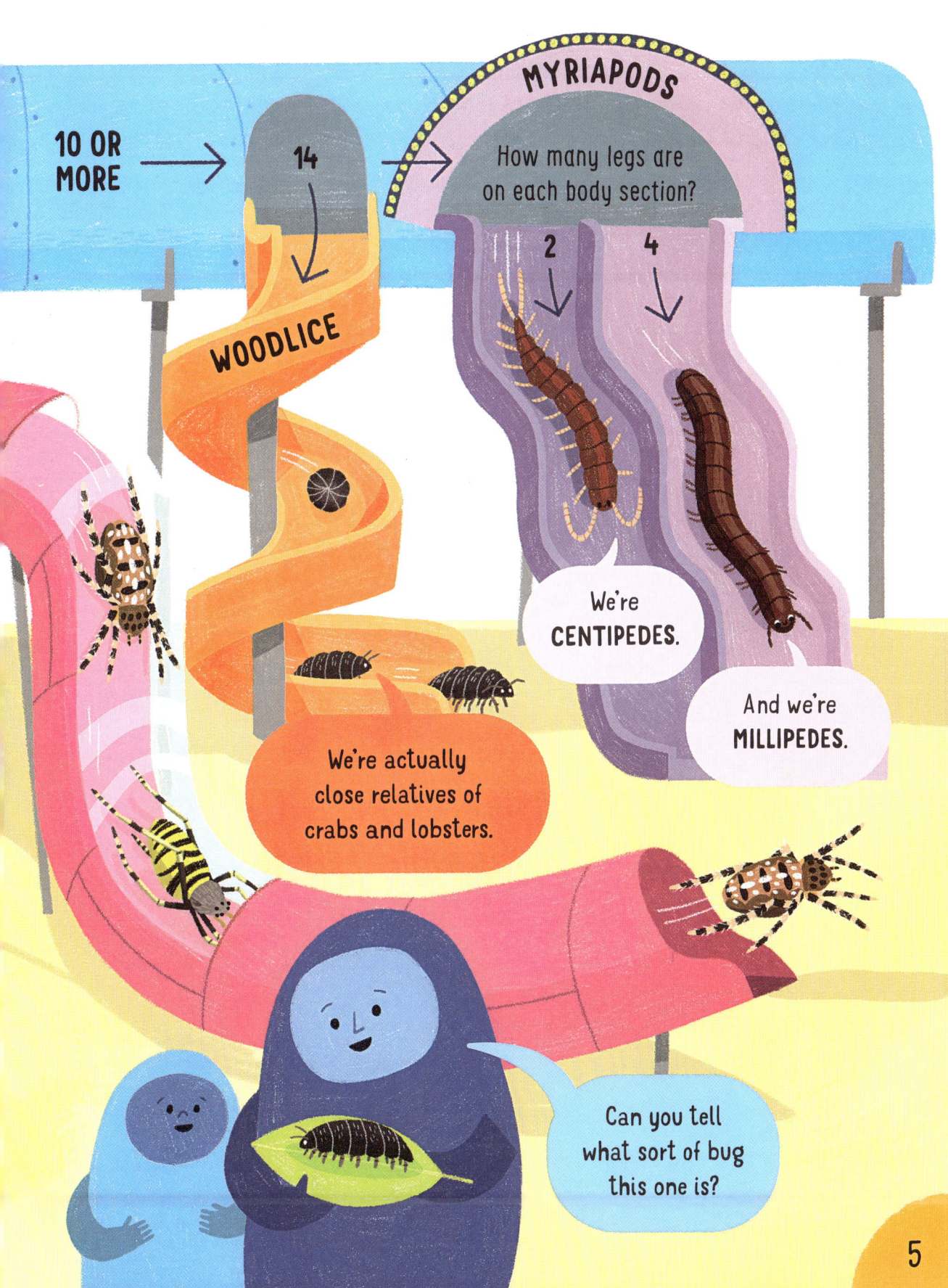

You'll never guess why fireflies glow

It's a warm summer night, and all around, fireflies are glowing. Romance is in the air...

Male fireflies flash their lights while flying.

Our lights help us find mates to start a family with.

Chemicals reacting in our bodies make us light up.

Females find a spot in the grass or on a bush.

If I enjoy the light show, I flash my light back to let the male know.

You'll never guess how many feet a millipede has

The name millipede means **'thousand feet'** in an ancient language called Latin. But do these wiggly, squiggly bugs **really** have that many?

Each of my body sections has four feet. So I have... 300 in total.

4 8 12 16 20 24 28 32 36 40 44 48 52...

Most millipedes, like this **giant African millipede**, have around **300** feet. This type of millipede can be as long as 30cm (12in).

Young millipedes have fewer feet than grown-up ones.

We grow more body sections – and legs – as we get older.

Amazing antennae

Did you know that bugs have two long noses on their heads that they can waggle about? These noses are called **antennae**.

Antennae noses are MUCH better at smelling things than human noses.

Having two antennae helps me tell which side a smell is coming from.

Long or hairy antennae are usually best at picking up smells.

My hairy antennae can sniff out a female moth from over 4km (2.5 miles) away.

WASP

LONGHORN BEETLE

ANT

POLYPHEMUS MOTH

But **antennae** aren't just for sniffing things out. Some bugs use their antennae to...

...sense hot and cold.

I'll close my wings to cool down, if I sense it's too hot.

Slurp

...tell how damp it is.

...feel the direction and strength of the wind.

Measuring the wind with my antennae helps me fly steadily.

...sense sounds.

I like low, buzzy sounds best.

...make sure there's nothing in their way — even when it's dark.

13

Changes

You probably don't look **SO** different from when you were a baby, but if you were a butterfly, you really would...

A butterfly starts life as an egg.

Then, a tiny caterpillar hatches.

It eats and eats, and grows and grows.

As it gets bigger, the caterpillar's skin becomes too tight. So, it sheds its skin, and grows a new one.

This happens FIVE times. Then, a hard pocket of skin called a **chrysalis** grows around the caterpillar.

Inside, the caterpillar changes. About ten days later, it comes out of the chrysalis...

...as a butterfly! This one is called a **red admiral**.

Lots of grown-up bugs looked **very** different as babies.

I was a GRUB for two weeks.

BUMBLEBEE

While I was growing, I was a NYMPH and I lived in water.

DRAGONFLY

I lived as a grub underground for three years, eating grass roots.

JUNE BUG

I couldn't fly back then...

LADYBIRD

They've all changed so much!

Spinning webs

Look out, flies! The sticky silk webs on these pages were all built by spiders to catch bugs like you to eat.

This is an **orb web**. Have you ever seen one? Orb-weaver spiders make a new one almost every day, in the same spot.

I recycle my old webs by eating them.

Silk is the name for the strong, thin threads that all kinds of spiders make.

Tangle space webs or **cobwebs** look messy. The threads run in all different directions.

Net-casting spiders weave small, sticky square nets. Then they throw these over small insects to catch them.

Once you fly in, it's impossible to get out. HELP!

If a fly bumps into one of the silky threads at the top of this web, it may well tumble down and get stuck on the **sheet web** below.

Funnel webs lie close to the ground. The spiders who build them hide deep inside, until they feel an insect land on their web...

I hang about under here until something falls in.

...then they pounce!

Spiders have other clever uses for their silk too.

Wheeee...

To travel long distances, spiders sometimes sail through the air on lines of silk. It's called **ballooning**.

My silk thread is like a rock climber's rope. It protects me from a big fall.

17

OUCH!

To find out more about insect stings, insect expert Justin Schmidt was stung at least a **thousand** times, by over a **hundred** different types of stinging bugs.

He invented the **Schmidt Pain Index** to compare different insect stings.

THE SCHMIDT PAIN INDEX

My sting feels explosive and long lasting, according to Schmidt. It makes people SCREAM in pain!

HUGE VELVET ANT — 3

The most painful sting of all comes from a **bullet ant**.

Schmidt said my sting was like walking over fire with a long nail in your heel!

4+

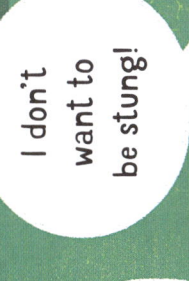

Dancing for their lives

Australian **peacock spiders** are tiny — about the size of a grain of rice — but they are big show-offs.

When a male peacock spider spots a female, he lifts up his bright body and two of his legs.

Then he fans out his body hair to make an eye-catching display.

As I dance, I make low, soothing noises called RUMBLE-RUMPS.

He moves about, waggling his legs and body in a funky dance.

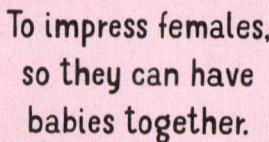

Why do they go to so much effort?

To impress females, so they can have babies together.

Plus, it's dangerous not to... If a female doesn't like the dance, she might eat him!

Ears all over

Can you imagine listening with your **KNEES**?

Katydids really do have ears on their knees.

My knee-ears are very good at telling where sounds come from. They help me find other katydids in the dark.

Lacewing ears are at the base of their wings.

And **grasshoppers** have ears on their bellies.

Some bugs don't have ears at all — but they can still hear you coming!

I hear sounds with my leg hairs — noises make them wobble.

23

The caterpillar needs to eat a **lot**, because once it becomes a moth, it won't eat at all.

My mouth is tiny, and doesn't actually work for eating.

Atlas moths don't live for long as moths. After a week or two, they run out of energy to flap their huge wings, and they die.

They leave behind more than a hundred eggs, which hatch around 65 days later into new caterpillars.

Grown by bugs

It's hard to believe, but if there weren't any insects, we wouldn't have **any** of these foods.

What do these foods have to do with insects?

They all contain plants that need insects' help to make seeds and fruits.

An incredible **three quarters** of all the plants we eat are helped by insects.

How bees talk

Honey bee nests are busy, buzzy places. There can be as many as 80,000 bees buzzing in and out! It would be pretty noisy if they talked like we do. Luckily, they don't...

The main way bees talk is by using SMELLS. Pop these antennae on so you can smell what they're saying.

This smell is only made by one bee — the nest's **queen**.

I'm in charge here. Get to work, loyal subjects!

The queen's smell tells the other bees to work hard. It also makes a group of bees stay close by, to feed and clean her.

Baby bees make a special smell too.

Feed us!

28

Near the entrance to the nest, bees make a lemony smell. It helps bees find their way home.

Here's the nest. COME HOME!

Bees fan their wings to spread the smell.

If a **guard** bee spots an intruder, she raises the alarm with a smell like ripe bananas.

I need back-up!
Come ready to sting.

WASP

Forager bees collect nectar from flowers and bring it back to the nest to make honey. They show each other the way to nectar by **DANCING**.

First the bee moves in the direction of the nectar, waggling its body.

waggle

Then it walks around to repeat the dance. It waggles and turns left, then it waggles and turns right, making the shape of a number 8.

If the nectar is a long way away, the bee waggles for longer.

29

Record-breaking insects

The insects on these pages all have a claim to fame...

The **horned dung beetle** isn't only the **strongest insect** — it's the world's **STRONGEST ANIMAL** for its size.

It can push a ball of dung more than a thousand times its own weight. That's like an adult shifting 13 elephants!

STRONGEST

SWOOOOOOOSH

The **FASTEST** insect in the world is the **dragonfly**. It can reach speeds of 56km (35 miles) an hour — faster than the fastest human runner.

FASTEST

The **LONGEST** insect in the world is **Phobaeticus chani**, a type of stick insect found in the rainforest of Borneo, Malaysia.

  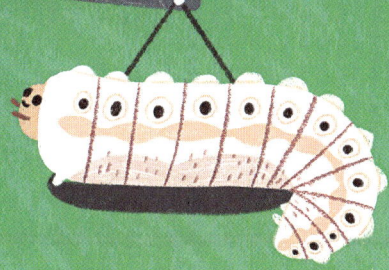

The **Goliath beetle** is the **HEAVIEST** insect. It can weigh as much as 60g (2oz) — that's around as much as a tennis ball.

It's even heavier when it's a baby. As a larva, it can weigh as much as 100g (3.5oz).

The **DEADLIEST** insect isn't poisonous, and it doesn't even have a sting — it's the **mosquito**.

In some parts of the world, mosquito bites can spread a disease called malaria. Around 600,000 people die of malaria every year.

Female chanis are 57cm (22 inches) long. The one shown here is actual size (but too long to fit on the page).

Welcome to the BUG FASHION SHOW!

Some talented bugs actually make costumes to wear. And tonight, I present to you a selection of these stylish outfits!

BAGWORM MOTH CATERPILLAR

This twig tower is a wearable home. As the caterpillar grows, it adds sticks to make its home bigger.

This fabulous tube was built by a **case-building caddisfly larva**. It's made from whatever was nearby and glued together with sticky silk.

sand
shells
tree bark

Ooo...

Aaa...

Amazing!

Beware the bombardier beetle!

Here's an insect you definitely shouldn't mess with.

When a bombardier beetle feels threatened by another creature, it takes aim...

POP!

...and squirts boiling hot, stinky, disgusting juice from its bottom.

How come the beetle doesn't burn itself?

The juice is made from two chemicals, which are stored separately inside the beetle. The chemicals only get hot when they mix together as they're squirted out.

34

Feet that taste

Humans taste with their tongues, but butterflies don't have tongues...

Butterflies have long tube-like mouths called **proboscises**. They look like this.

I unroll my proboscis and use it like a straw to suck sweet nectar out of flowers.

But a proboscis can't actually taste much. Instead of using its mouth to taste, a butterfly uses its **feet**.

When I'm looking for a plant to lay eggs on, my feet taste whether it would be good for my baby caterpillars to eat.

What do my fingers taste like to you?

35

300 million years ago...

...long, long before humans or even dinosaurs existed, **giant creepy-crawlies** scuttled, squirmed and swooped all over Planet Earth.

There were **dragonflies** the size of seagulls.

These dragonflies had sharp teeth and spikes on their legs for grabbing hold of creatures to eat in the air.

Argh!

Some **millipedes** were as long as cars. Scientists don't know for sure whether they ate plants or hunted other creatures.

Ancient bugs left behind rock-like traces called fossils. That's how we know they existed.

This bug, called **Mazothairos**, was almost as large as a pigeon.

Some dragonfly fossils are around 300 million years old.

Quick, back to the time machine.

37

EXTREME BUGS

These bugs may just be the bravest creatures on Earth. They live in some of the harshest places on Earth and do things you wouldn't dare...

There's only one animal that spends all its life on frozen Antarctica... the tiny **Antarctic midge**.

ANTIFREEZE chemicals in my blood stop me from freezing.

Most creatures flee a forest fire, but **charcoal beetles** are drawn to the heat.

In the Sahara Desert, the sand is hot enough to cook an egg — or an insect. But that doesn't stop **Sahara Desert ants**...

We run REALLY fast when we're outside our nest, so we don't bake.

We lay our eggs in freshly burned trees.

38

Bugs to discover

Scientists have already discovered more than a **million** different types of bug. But they think there are many more still to discover.

There could be as many as **10 MILLION** different types of bug on Earth.

Around 8,000 new types are discovered EVERY year.

This longhorn beetle was found in Australia in 2024.

I'm quite hard to spot, because my white hairs make me look like bird poo.

Do you think I could discover a new type of bug?

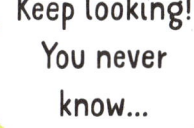

Keep looking! You never know...

39

Walking on water

Pond skaters have an extraordinary talent — they can walk on water.

We can stand perfectly still on water, too.

Pond skaters float because of tiny waterproof hairs all over their feet.

Without these, they'd soak up water and slowly sink, like this poor fly.

There's a fly in the water. I can tell from the ripples.

...helping them to spot when a tasty insect falls in.

It's actually more like skating. We can zip around INCREDIBLY fast.

Pond skaters' hairy feet have another use, too. They can sense tiny movements on the water's surface...

Pond skaters aren't the only bugs you'll find at a pond...

Water boatmen spend their lives in the water, but they still need to breathe air.

So, they take a bubble of air down from the surface. Hairs on their tummy stop the bubble from floating away.

Diving bell spiders build their webs underwater.

They have hairy bottoms, which they use to collect bubbles of air. They trap bubbles in their webs, to breathe later.

There's enough air here for more for than a day.

Beetle worship

Thousands of years ago, people in ancient Egypt worshipped a god who they painted with a **dung beetle** head.

I am KHEPRI, god of the rising Sun.

According to ancient Egyptian legends, every day Khepri pushed the Sun across the sky, then buried it in the evening...

...just like a dung beetle rolls a ball of dung along the ground, then buries it to eat later.

The Day of the Dead

Every year, a flurry of **monarch butterflies** arrives in Mexico. They fly in at the start of November — just in time for the Day of the Dead festival.

We fly in from Canada and the USA, to spend the winter in Mexico, where it's warmer.

Then in spring, we fly north again.

Millions of us make this journey every year.

The Day of the Dead involves street parties and parades. Some people believe that the butterflies are the spirits of relatives returning for the party.

Sometimes we dress up as monarch butterflies as part of the celebrations.

Insects in disguise

Some bugs blend in so well with their surroundings that they're incredibly hard to spot.

A **stick insect** looks like a twig or branch. This disguise keeps it hidden from things that may want to eat it.

Here I am!

An **orchid mantis** may look like a pretty flower, but it's vicious.

When butterflies or bugs come along, I pounce. DELICIOUS!

"I'm hard to spot among the leaves."

LEAF INSECT

ORANGE OAKLEAF BUTTERFLY

"My wings are bright and beautiful..."

"...but when I close them, I look like a boring, old dead leaf."

If a hungry bird starts chasing the butterfly, it closes its wings and drops to the ground.

"The bird won't find me here. I'm perfectly disguised."

45

Hard on the outside

Your skeleton is under your skin, but most bugs wear theirs as a hard case on the outside. It's called an **exoskeleton**.

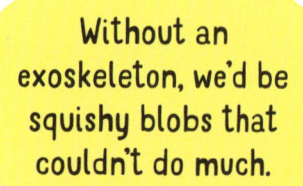

Without an exoskeleton, we'd be squishy blobs that couldn't do much.

Our hard cases also help protect us from hungry animals.

Some cases are **incredibly** tough.

The **ironclad beetle** has a case so hard, that a car can drive over it without damaging it.

I'm fine!

But having a hard outer case makes one thing **very** difficult — growing.

When a bug gets too big for its exoskeleton, it grows a new one underneath then takes off the old one.

Shedding an old case is rather tricky. Sometimes bugs lose a leg or get stuck and die.

46

Ready for battle

Male **rhinoceros beetles** have a built-in weapon.

They have MASSIVE horns!

They use their horns to grip, lift and throw each other, as they fight to be noticed by female beetles.

This type of rhinoceros beetle is called the HERCULES BEETLE, after a super strong hero from Ancient Greek and Roman myths.

Hercules beetles can be as long as 19cm (7.5 inches).

A fly's eye view

Flies see the world very differently from the way you do. It's all to do with the strange way their bug eyes work.

Bug eyes are made of lots and lots of mini eyes.

Each dot on this housefly's two big eyes is a mini eye. It has **thousands**, all pointing in different directions.

HOUSEFLY

That means the fly sees pictures made up of thousands of different parts, like this...

The pictures aren't as sharp as the pictures humans see. But, because their eyes point in almost every direction, they show what's going on **all around** the fly.

Flies' eyes work about four times faster than human eyes.

So, flies notice things coming their way a lot sooner than you would.

That's what makes it so hard to catch a fly.

Because our eyes work faster, movements that look quick to humans seem REEEALLY slow to us.

We have plenty of time to fly away.

49

The noisy bug orchestra

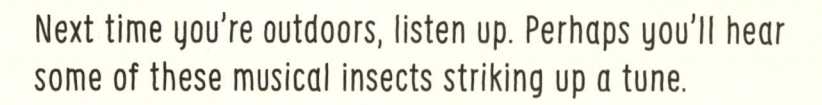

Next time you're outdoors, listen up. Perhaps you'll hear some of these musical insects striking up a tune.

Male **cicadas** are the loudest bugs of all.

CROAK

1, 2, 3.
1, 2, 3...

We make music by vibrating our hollow, drum-like bodies.

If a **click beetle** gets stuck upside down, it pops its back with a loud...

CLICK

This bounces it back onto its feet.

SQUEEEAAAAAKK

Scientists think **death's head hawk moths** squeak to frighten animals that might want to eat them.

50

A **bumblebee**'s buzz is actually the sound of its wings flapping.

BUZZZZZZZZZZZZ

Male **crickets** chirp by rubbing their wings together.

CHIRP CHIRP CHIRP

Our chirping lets females know we'd like to meet them.

PRRRRRR PRRRR PRRRRR

There's no cat here... That purring noise comes from this **wolf spider** shaking a leaf. It does this to impress other wolf spiders.

Invented by insects

Bugs have inspired humans to come up with some amazing creations...

PAPER, INSPIRED BY WASPS

Paper used to be made from fabric or leather — and was **very** expensive.

Then, in 1719, René Antoine Ferchault de Réaumur saw wasps chewing up wood and using it to build a papery nest.

If wasps can make paper from chewed-up wood, maybe humans could too...

His idea caught on. By 1850, mushed-up wood was one of the main ingredients in paper. This was an easy way to make much cheaper paper.

MEDICINES, FIRST USED BY ANTS

Lots of ants make their own medicine, using tiny things called bacteria that live on their bodies.

Scientists are looking at ways to use these ant medicines to help sick humans.

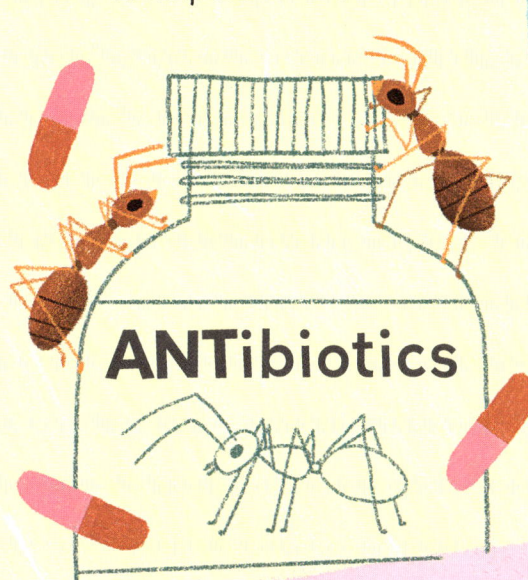

ANTibiotics

MINI ROBOTS, MODELLED ON BEES

Lots of the plants we eat wouldn't grow if bees didn't visit their flowers.

Technology companies are trying to build robot-bees that can visit flowers and spread their pollen like bees do.

CHAINSAW, BASED ON PONDEROUS BORER LARVAE

Ponderous borer larvae have curved teeth which they move from side to side to cut through wood easily.

In the 1940s, Joseph Buford Cox designed a chainsaw with teeth that cut like these larvae. It was **far** better at cutting wood than previous designs.

53

Spot the difference

There are around 5,000 different types of ladybirds, with all kinds of patterns. Look at all the ones just on this page...

Most ladybirds have bright and spotty wing cases...

...but not all of us.

In some countries, people think seeing a ladybird is lucky.

Our bright colours help keep us safe. They warn hungry animals that we taste really yucky.

Did you know, the name for a group of ladybirds is a LOVELINESS.

They do look lovely...

Why there's a fly on this painting

A surprising number of old paintings have realistic-looking flies painted on them...

Shoo!

Ha ha!

Why won't it fly away?

That's not a real fly – I painted it!

Painted flies like this were little jokes, designed to trick people.

They were also a way for artists to show off just how talented they were at painting details in the world around them.

You'll never guess who built these...

In the scorching deserts of Australia, huge earthy towers rise out of the ground.

Some of these are more than twice as tall as a grown-up.

Amazingly, these massive mounds are built by tiny ant-like creatures called **cathedral termites**.

Here's what one looks like inside.

The tower acts as an air-conditioning system.

Chimneys suck in cool air, to keep the temperature inside just right.

FOOD STORE

NURSERY

The termites live in a nest at the base of the mound.

How can something so small build something so ENORMOUS?

By working together!

We chew up mud, grass and our own poo...

...and mix it up with our spit...

...then pile it up.

Building a new tower can take as long as **FIVE YEARS**. But once up, it may stand for as long as **100 YEARS**.

Meet the bug recycling team

Without these recycling heroes, there would be dead plants and animals piled high EVERYWHERE — and lots of poo as well!

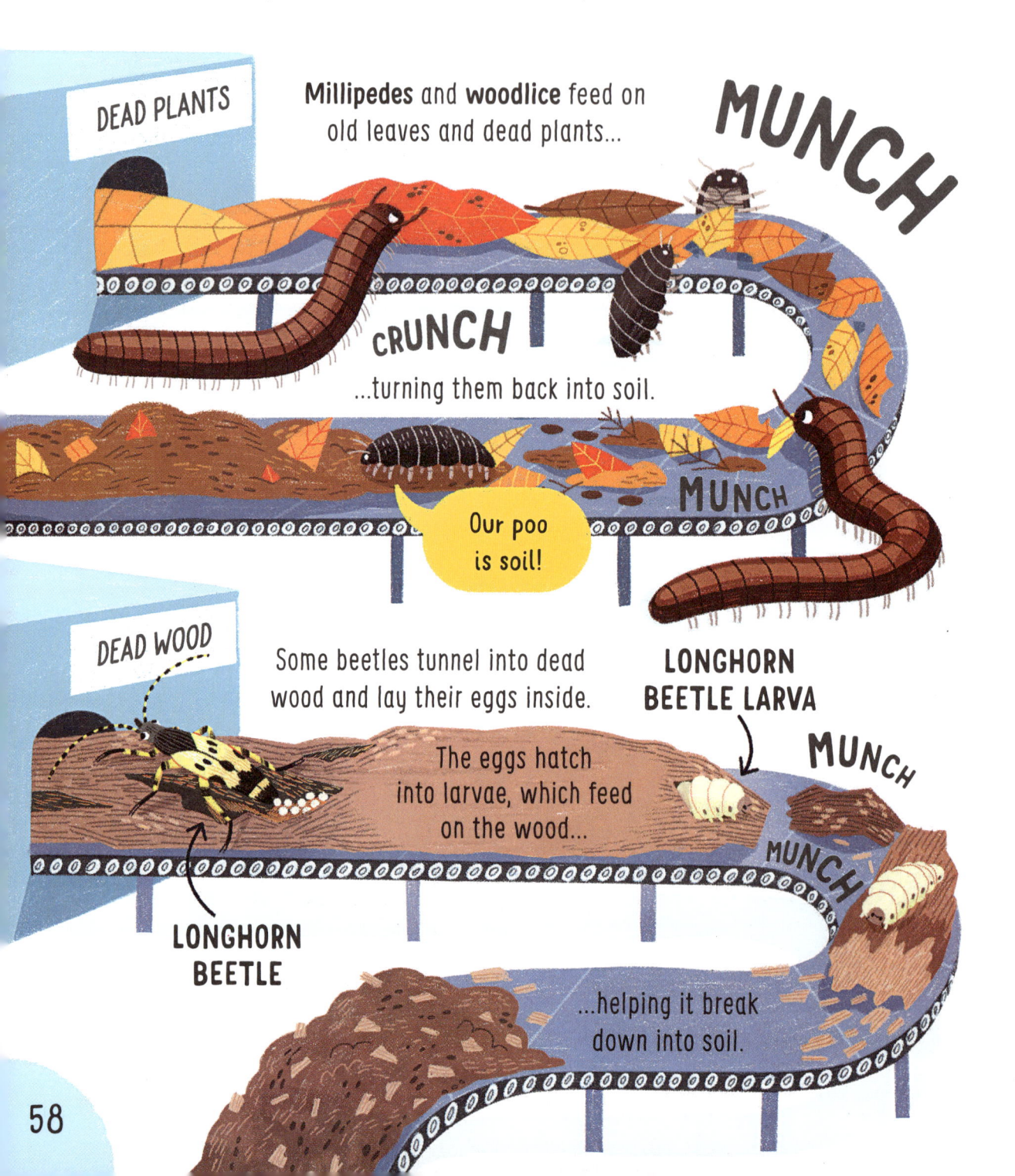

DEAD PLANTS

Millipedes and **woodlice** feed on old leaves and dead plants...

MUNCH

CRUNCH

...turning them back into soil.

MUNCH

Our poo is soil!

DEAD WOOD

Some beetles tunnel into dead wood and lay their eggs inside.

LONGHORN BEETLE LARVA

The eggs hatch into larvae, which feed on the wood...

MUNCH

MUNCH

LONGHORN BEETLE

...helping it break down into soil.

DEAD ANIMALS

All sorts of bugs help tidy up when animals die — by eating them.

Burying beetles, or **Sexton beetles**, actually bury them as well.

I'll lay my eggs on this dead mouse. There's lots for my babies to eat.

Just one cow makes 15 huge cowpats every day. Luckily, **dung beetles** know what to do with it.

DUNG

Some roll balls of it away...

...others set up home in the dung...

Home Sweet Home

...and others dig down under the dung and bury balls of it.

They all eat dung and turn it back into soil.

59

How you can help bugs

Bugs do so much for us — they tidy up dead plants, help grow our food and they are food themselves for other amazing creatures.

Here are some ways you can say **thank you**.

Spread the bug love by telling friends and family the amazing things you know about bugs.

Did you know...

Lots of types of butterflies, bees and other bugs aren't as common as they once were. Bugs need your help!

Maybe you could become a scientist and find out more about bugs, or discover a new type.

Oooooo...

Sow flowers for the bugs.

Mmmm...

Don't squash us! Take us outside, instead.

If you have an outdoor space at home or school, you could...

...grow flowers that bugs love.

CHIVES   MARIGOLDS   LAVENDER

YARROW

...pile up wood for bugs to live in.

...or leave a patch to grow wild.

Yum!

Long grass is better for us.

61

Glossary

Here you can find out what some of the words in this book *mean*...

antennae — the two waggly parts on a bug's head that sense smells and do all sorts of other jobs.

caterpillar — the wiggly, wingless baby form of butterflies and moths. It's a type of *larva*.

chrysalis — a hard pocket of skin a butterfly caterpillar grows to protect it while it changes into a butterfly.

cocoon — a pocket made from *silk* by moth caterpillars and some other insects to protect them while they change into their adult form.

exoskeleton — a hard case bugs have on the outside, which holds them together.

grub — a name for a bug that isn't yet a grown-up.

insect — bugs with a head, two other body parts and six legs. There are lots of different types.

larva — a name for a baby bug.

myriapods — the name scientists give to bugs with lots of legs. Centipedes and millipedes are myriapods.

nectar — a sweet liquid made by flowers. Some bees, butterflies and other bugs drink it.

nymph — the name for some baby bugs, such as baby dragonflies and grasshoppers.

pollen — a yellow powder made by flowers. Bees and other insects carry it from plant to plant, which helps flowers grow fruits and seeds.

proboscis — a long tube-like mouth used for sucking.

rumble-rump — a low, soothing noise made by a male peacock spider to impress a female spider.

silk — strong threads made by spiders and some baby bugs, such as moth caterpillars.

sting — a sharp point at the end of the body of a bee, wasp or ant, which the bug uses to inject *venom* if it feels threatened.

venom — the name for a poison made by an insect or animal.

web — a mesh of fine *silk* threads built by a spider to catch bugs to eat.

Index

ancient bugs, 36–37
ancient Egyptians, 42
antennae, 12–13, 28, 62
ants, 4, 12, 18–19, 20, 38, 53, 56

baby bugs, 14–15, 28, 31, 35
bees, 15, 21, 27, 28–29, 51, 53, 60
beetles, 3, 4, 12, 30–31, 33, 34, 38, 39, 42, 46, 47, 53, 58–59
   bombardier, 34
   dung, 30, 42, 59
   Goliath, 31
   ladybird, 15, 54
   longhorn, 12, 39, 58
   rhinoceros, 47
bug-eating plants, 10–11
bumblebees, 15, 51
butterflies, 4, 14, 27, 35, 43, 44, 45, 60
   growing up, 14
   monarch, 43
   red admiral, 14
   tasting, 35

caterpillars, 2, 3, 14, 24–25, 32, 35, 62
centipedes, 5
chrysalis, 14, 62
cicadas, 50
cocoons, 2, 62
crickets, 4, 51

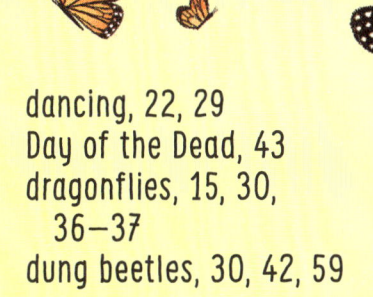

dancing, 22, 29
Day of the Dead, 43
dragonflies, 15, 30, 36–37
dung beetles, 30, 42, 59

ears, 23
eating, 14, 15, 16, 18, 22, 24–25, 35, 36, 58–59
eggs, 14, 25, 35, 58–59
exoskeletons, 46, 62
eyes, 48–49

fireflies, 6–7
flies, 4, 10–11, 13, 16–17, 40, 48–49, 55
food (helping grow), 26–27, 60

Goliath beetles, 31
grasshoppers, 4, 23
grubs, 15, 62

honey bee, 21, 28–29
housefly, 48–49

insects, 4, 10, 16–17, 19, 20–21, 26–27, 30–31, 34, 38, 40, 44–45, 50–51, 52, 62
   leaf, 45
   stick, 30–31, 44

June bugs, 15
junk bugs, 33

katydids, 23
Khepri, 42

lacewings, 23
ladybirds, 15, 54
larvae, 31, 32–33, 53, 58, 62
leaf insects, 45
longhorn beetles, 12, 39, 58

mantises, 3, 44
medicine, 53
midges, 38
millipedes, 5, 8–9, 36, 58
mosquitos, 31
moths, 2, 4, 12, 24–25, 32, 50
mouths, 10, 25, 35
myriapods, 5, 62
   centipedes, 5
   millipedes, 5, 8–9, 36, 58

63

nectar, 19, 27, 29, 35, 62
nests, 18, 28–29, 38, 52, 56–57
noses, 12, 21
nymphs, 15, 33, 62

paintings, 55
plants, 10–11, 26–27, 33, 35, 36, 53, 58, 60
pollen, 27, 53, 62
pond skaters, 40
proboscises, 35, 62

rhinoceros beetle, 47
rumble-rumps, 22, 62

silk, 16–17, 32, 62
smells, 10–11, 12, 28–29, 33, 34
spiders, 4–5, 16–17, 22, 23, 41, 51, 60
webs, 16–17, 41, 62
spittlebug nymphs, 33
stick insects, 30–31, 44
stings, 19, 20–21, 29, 31, 62

termites, 56–57

venus fly traps, 10

wasps, 4, 12, 21, 29, 52
water boatmen, 41
webs, 16–17, 41, 62
woodlice, 5, 58

Series editor: Ruth Brocklehurst
Series designer: Helen Lee

First published in 2025 by Usborne Publishing Limited, 83-85 Saffron Hill, London EC1N 8RT, United Kingdom. usborne.com Copyright © 2025 Usborne Publishing Limited. The name Usborne and the Balloon logo are registered trade marks of Usborne Publishing Limited. All rights reserved. No part of this publication may be reproduced, stored in a retrieval system or transmitted in any form or by any means without prior permission of the publisher. UKE.

Please follow the online safety guidelines at usborne.com/Quicklinks

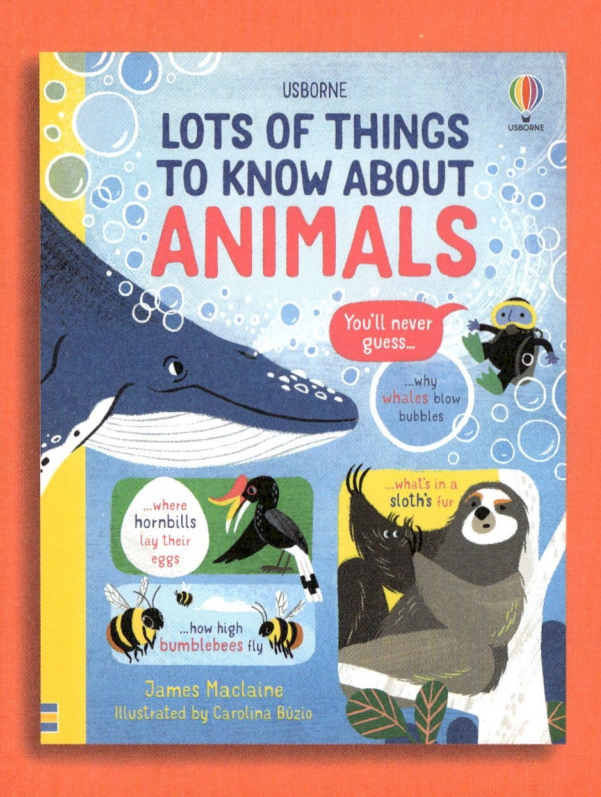

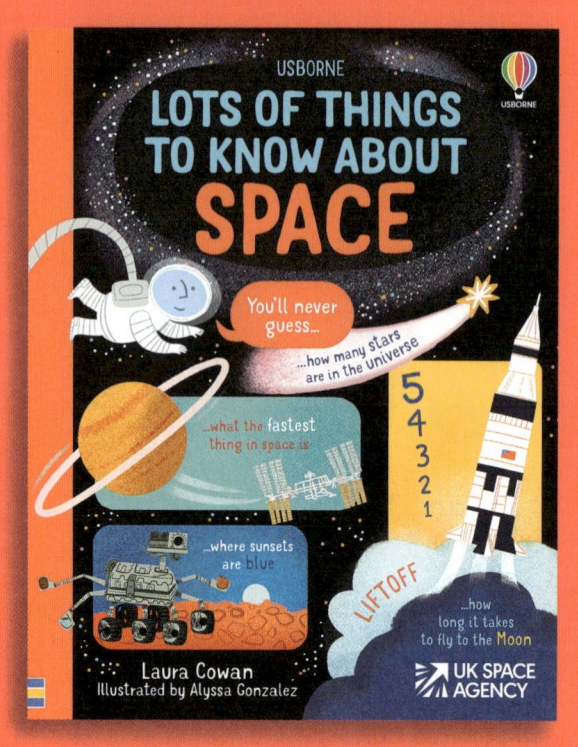

There are lots and lots more things to know!

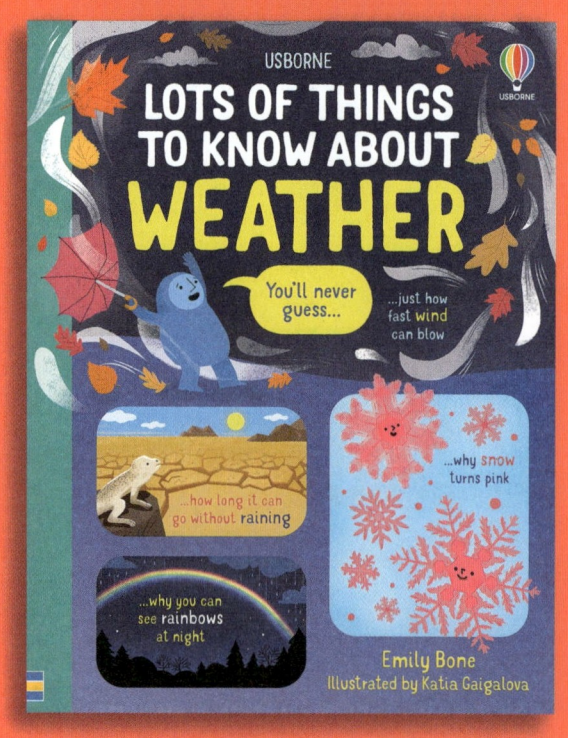